MW00977109

Glory

Bringing about True Unity in the Body of Christ

By

Julia Eileen McLaughlin

Arise, shine; for your light has come!

And the glory of the Lord is risen upon you.

For behold, the darkness shall cover the earth,

and deep darkness the people;

But the Lord will arise over you,

And His glory will be seen upon you.

The Gentiles shall come to your light,

And kings to the brightness of your rising.

Isaiah 60:1-3

Table of Contents

"They shall see the Son of man coming in power and great glory." [Luke 21:27] "The Son of man shall come in His glory, and all holy angels with Him." [Matthew 25:31] Christ will return – not in humility; not as a babe in Bethlehem's manger; not to be wrapped in swaddling bands, not to be mocked and scoffed and spit upon; not to die on a cross; not to lie buried in a stranger's tomb; but – in glory and accompanied by all heaven's angelic host.

- Harvey McAlister in 1929

One of the five founders of the Pentecostal Assemblies of Canada,

Attendee of the Azusa Street Holy Spirit outpouring in the early 1900's,

Founder of the famous Stone Church in Toronto, Canada and numerous other churches throughout North America,

One of the editors of the Voice of Healing magazine,

Worldwide healing evangelist who traveled to more than 50 countries and preached a six-week evangelistic healing crusade in Hong Kong at age 75

(and my great-grandfather)

Introduction

I am on a mission to bring unity to the Body of Christ.

This sounds ambitious and, frankly, it is. However, if we do not start somewhere, then this generation, and the next, and perhaps even the next will be stuck going around this mountain again - continuing to wander around in the proverbial "wilderness" merely hoping that someday the Lord will return with a triumphant shout and call them home to heaven - the promised land.

The reality is I want to see that happen in my generation - in our generation - and why not? Why not do all we can to make that happen in this world while we are still alive on the earth to see it and can be called up to meet Him in the air?

It <u>IS</u> possible.

All the signs of our time point to this being the greatest season of potential for His return. Yet, there is at least one thing we know will absolutely be an indicator of His return and we are not yet seeing it happen on a mass scale throughout the earth.

The Body of Christ will function as a "body" with Christ as its Head in a way that will bring untold glory to Him so that millions, hopefully billions, more will know Him and His unquestioning, unconditional love for them.

From Ephesians 4:12-16 in the Amplified Bible, we learn:

> "His intention was the perfecting and the full equipping of the saints (His consecrated people), [that they should do] the work of ministering toward building up Christ's body (the church), [That it might develop] until we all attain oneness in the faith and in the comprehension of the [full and accurate] knowledge of the Son of God, that [we might arrive] at really mature manhood (the completeness of personality which is nothing less than the standard height of Christ's own perfection), the measure of the stature of the fullness of the Christ and the completeness found in Him... For because of Him the whole body (the church, in all its various parts), closely joined and firmly knit together by the joints and ligaments with which it is supplied, when each part [with power adapted to its need] is working properly [in all its functions], grows to full maturity, building itself up in love." (AMP)

People, if we have any hope of His return, we must begin to function well together - as one - not with false unity, but with true unity that only He can pour out on His people through the glory - His glory - that He left for us and that we have almost lost sight of in the earth.

Yet my mission cannot be accomplished alone.

You and I are but two of billions who have the opportunity to fulfill this mission together in our generation.

Will you join me on this, the greatest of all adventures?

We need to get back to the simplicity and unity of the early church.

- John Roach Straton in 1920

> Nationally known fundamentalist pastor of the famous Calvary Baptist Church in New York City with prior pastorates in Chicago, Baltimore, and Norfolk
>
> Installed the first church-owned radio station in the United States,
>
> Defender of Aimee Semple McPherson nationally from the pulpit during her trial,
>
> Experienced a Pentecostal outpouring of the Holy Spirit at his flagship Baptist church in New York City in 1927 and began holding healing services there and around the country
>
> (and my great-grandfather)

Glory: Bringing about True Unity in the Body of Christ

Chapter 1

The Mission
The Importance of Unity

Let's take a few moments to unpack this concept of why unity is important.

After more than twenty years in the corporate world, I greatly appreciate the business principle of "Begin with the End in Mind". Many people know that it comes from a popular leadership book by Stephen Covey; however, I find the phrase quite applicable to our walk with Christ and our development into the full stature of the Body of Christ.

Therefore, with this principle of "Begin with the End in Mind", we look to the Word of God found in the Bible and to Jesus, Our Lord and Savior - the Author and Finisher of our faith.

For He also began with the end in mind -

> From Isaiah 46:9-10: "...for I am God, and there is no other; I am God, and there is none like Me, declaring the end from the beginning, and from ancient times things that are not yet done..."

> From Titus 1:2: "eternal life which God, who cannot lie, promised before time began"

> From Revelation 22:13: "... I am the Alpha and the Omega, the Beginning and the End, the First and the Last."

So, as we seek to accomplish our mission of the Lord's return in our generation, we need to discover what will bring Him back.

Through the Church ages, we have been taught as Christians that Christ will return for us - His beautiful, spotless Bride – the Body of Christ. Yet I look around at our people – our brothers and sisters in Christ – my fellow Christians – around the world, across all denominations, and throughout all the centuries since His departure and wonder what will He come back to?

Who is this Bride for whom the Lord will return?

We are the most bedraggled, worn out, confused, selfish, backstabbing, self-wounding "bride" that any bridegroom could ever be saddled with. I get it - His grace covers us and because we are helpless and hopeless in our unrighteousness He is able to make us appear as spotless individuals to the Father through His blood poured out for us at Calvary. But seriously - there are days when I just want to shout from the hills to all those who profess the Lord as their Savior and King:

> "People, we can do better than this! Really! We can! Let's at least help ourselves prepare for His return. After all, who would want to marry us in our current condition? Certainly not the King of Kings and Lord of Lords, right?"

Seriously, I have a hard time believing this Person...

> From Revelation 19:11-16: "Now I saw heaven opened, and behold, a white horse. And He who sat on him was called Faithful and True, and in righteousness He judges and makes war. His eyes were like a flame of fire, and on His head were many crowns. He had a name written that no one knew except Himself. He was clothed with a robe dipped in blood, and His name is called The Word of God... And He has on His robe and on His thigh a name written: KING OF KINGS AND LORD OF LORDS."

Or this one - the same Person...

> From Ezekiel 1:26-28: "there was something that looked like a throne, sky-blue like a sapphire, with a humanlike figure towering above the throne. From what I could see from the waist up he looked like burnished bronze and from the waist down like a blazing fire. Brightness everywhere! The way a rainbow springs out of the sky on a rainy day – that's what it was like. It turned out to be the Glory of God!" (MSG)

... would want to return to marry the bride that we see among ourselves as the Body of Christ.

Jesus, King of Kings and Lord of Lords, is completely interested in us as individuals, but He is not interested in us collectively as His Bride if we cannot work together to stand beside Him, fight beside Him, and rescue the lost with Him in order to ultimately rule and reign throughout eternity by His side.

There is literally no scenario where He would want a childish, petty, disheveled, self-centered, self-righteous heap of a wife who was not strong enough to stand up for herself, help herself, not stab herself, not cut off her own body parts, not reject herself, and ultimately not help her Husband. Yet that is what we have become as the "church" universal. We are barely able to hold ourselves together in order to agree on the basics and certainly not able to fully minister to the lost on the mass scale that Christ envisioned when He prayed to the Father in John 17:20 - 21:

> "that they all may be one, as You, Father, are in Me, and I in You; that they also may be one in Us, that the world may believe that You sent Me."

Or further on in that passage where Christ continues:

> "that they may be one just as We are one: I in them, You in Me; that they may be made perfect in one, and that the world may know that You have sent Me, and have loved them as You have loved Me." John 17: 22b – 23

You see - this is why UNITY IS IMPORTANT - because unity, true unity with Christ as the head of the Church and each of us fully functioning as the part we are designed to be, brings about the Body of Christ – the Bride – and demonstrates to the world the Father's love for lost and broken humanity.

This gospel - the true gospel - that God so loved the world that He gave His only begotten Son to save the world - must be preached throughout the earth, with full demonstration, so that all may have the opportunity to choose Christ, and then the end will come.

> From John 3:16: "This is how much God loved the world: He gave his Son, his one and only Son. And this is why: so that no one need be destroyed; by believing in Him anyone can have a whole and lasting life."(MSG)

> From Matthew 24:14: "And this gospel of the kingdom will be preached in all the world as a witness to all the nations, and then the end will come."

And let me be clear again - this is NOT a false unity, this is NOT a manufactured unity, and this is NOT the unity of denominations or ministerial associations.

This is true unity in submission to Christ, guided by the Holy Spirit, and validated through the Word of God given to us in the Bible. This is the true unity found among believers in Christ around the world - beyond denominations, beyond manufactured differences, beyond artificial interpretations, beyond the boundaries established by people. This is the unity of the early church - the unity

Christ left to us in order for us to be built up into the beautiful, strong, healthy, glorious Bride that He would return to marry.

So my mission for bringing unity to the Body of Christ is quite selfish - I want Him to return in my generation, in our generation. I want to be part of His glorious, strong, healthy, fully functional bride, who is ready for His return. I want to see Him split the eastern sky and return on a white horse to meet her and usher in eternity.

But how do we become that Bride – the one for whom He wants to return? By what mechanism will we be brought into full alignment as a Body – His Bride – who can rule and reign with Him?

(Hint: It's not through holding conferences, weekend retreats, church camps, camp meetings, mission trips, or having other church-y moments, but those are important and fun for other reasons!)

Christ, for the specific purpose of procuring man's redemption allowed all the glory, possessed originally with the Father, to be veiled from the view of man by becoming incarnate. He threw a robe of flesh about Himself, as it were, and walked among men. The Son of God became the Son of man in order that we, sons [and daughters] of men, might become the sons [and daughters] of God and share with Him in His glory.

- Harvey McAlister in 1929

One of the five founders of the Pentecostal Assemblies of Canada,

Attendee of the Azusa Street Holy Spirit outpouring in the early 1900's,

Founder of the famous Stone Church in Toronto, Canada and numerous other churches throughout North America,

One of the editors of the Voice of Healing magazine,

Worldwide healing evangelist who traveled to more than 50 countries and preached a six-week evangelistic healing crusade in Hong Kong at age 75

(and my great-grandfather)

Chapter 2

The Mechanism
Christ's Gift of Glory that Generates True Unity (and More!)

True unity does not happen by chance or coincidence or blind luck.

True unity does not happen because we have a natural affinity for someone, or because we like their personality, or because we agree with them on intellectual or theological matters.

True unity transcends all of that. True unity is generated by a mechanism – more like a substance – that flows from the throne room of heaven and is poured out on the people of earth.

Christ is quite clear in His prayer to God the Father about what generates true unity. Stuck right in the middle of Christ's prayer at the end of John 17 is a relatively short, but extremely important verse.

In John 17:22, He says,

"And the **glory** which You gave Me I have given them"

and He goes on to state that this gift of the Father's glory – this substance that bonds us to Him and to each other – is given to us with the purpose of bringing about unity – true unity:

"that they may be one just as We are one".

He is literally explaining to God the Father in words recorded for our reference throughout eternity that He, Christ Jesus, gave us the glory He had received from the Father in order that we would be one with Him and with each other just as He is one with the Father.

And in John 17:23, He reiterates our relationship with Him and goes on to describe this and two additional reasons for this gift of His Glory:

"I in them, and You in Me;

that they may be made perfect in one,

and that the world may know that You [God the Father] have sent Me [Jesus Christ],

and have loved them [humanity] as You have loved Me."

So this gift - the Father's glory - was freely given by Christ to us for three reasons.

According to John 17:22 & 23, those three reasons are:

1. Unity - That we may be one, and not just one, but "perfect in one"

2. Authority - That the world would know (and not doubt) that God the Father sent Jesus Christ, His Son

3. Testimony - That the world would know (and not doubt) that God the Father loves humanity – every person, individually, regardless of their current state of depravity or greatness

While you take a moment to reflect on the incredible awesomeness of this gift – God's own glory – accessible to us by His only Son,

- Ask yourself – what are we doing with the glory He has given each of us?
- Is His glory activated in our lives daily?
- Are we actively using it to reflect His light and love and, more importantly, to draw all people to Him?

And then, prepare to dive deep into the value of this amazing gift!

Here we go...

...and is the bride of Christ a mere abstraction? Is it an abstraction that Christ loved and gave himself for, that he might sanctify and cleanse it with the washing of water by the word? It was not an abstraction that he designed to perfect and present to himself. He did not expend his love and sufferings to perfect the ecclesiastical institution. Nor was it his design to perfect the instituted churches, and present them to himself as a glorious family of churches. The object to be presented is a church.

The bride, the Lamb's wife, is but one.

- John Leadley (J. L.) Dagg, in 1858, from the *Manual of Theology Second Part: A Treatise on Church Order* written for the Baptist denomination

Author of the *Manual of Theology* – the first comprehensive, systematic theology written by a Baptist in America – as well as *Moral Science* and *Evidences of Christianity*,

One of the most respected and profound thinkers in the Baptist Denomination,

Third president of Mercer University,

Soldier in the War of 1812

(and my fourth great-grandfather)

Chapter 3

The Value
True <u>Unity</u> - Our Ultimate Destiny Revealed

Psalm 133 begins with the verse "Behold, how good and how pleasant it is for brethren to dwell together in unity!" and woven throughout the scriptures we find that God is about bringing a people into unity to worship Him for all eternity. The personal, individual story of the Bible is one of God redeeming each person through the power of His love and willingness to sacrifice His only begotten Son to atone for the sins of each of us. Yet there is a greater macro-story and, again, we see it when we examine the end of The Story:

From Revelation 22:17: "The Spirit and the bride say, "Come!"

And who is "the bride" mentioned in that verse? She is described throughout Revelation 21:9-27 after one of the angels says to John, "Come, I will show you the bride, the Lamb's wife." John begins to describe her, Christ's wife, as "the great city, holy Jerusalem, descending out of heaven from God, having the <u>glory</u> of God."

Then he goes on to describe in detail what he sees of the city including pearls as gates and streets of pure gold (Seriously, who would not want to live there!), and towards the end of this passage John describes perhaps the most important aspect of the city – the Source of its illumination and its inhabitants:

From Revelation 21:23-24: "The city had no need of the sun or of the moon to shine in it, for the glory of God illuminated it. The Lamb is its light. And the nations of those who are saved shall walk in its light..."

We are given great insight in this passage, for it describes that the Lamb's wife is made up not only of the physical city descending from heaven, but also of the inhabitants who are saved through the Lamb and walk in His light – the glory of God.

Clearly those of us who are saved are those inhabitants who make up "the bride" and, as His bride, we are meant to walk in God's glory.

The wonderful aspect of walking in God's glory is also that Christ has made it clear that we do not have to wait until some future date or future world to walk in it. Both in the Old Testament and in the New Testament, we see confirmation that God's glory is accessible to us in the here and now.

Let's examine some of those passages by letting the pure Word of God speak directly to our hearts and minds:

> From Isaiah 60:1-3: "Arise, shine; for your light has come! And the glory of the Lord is risen upon you. For behold, the darkness shall cover the earth, and deep darkness the people; but the Lord will arise over you, and His glory will be seen upon you."
>
> From Psalm 85:9: "Surely His salvation is near to those who fear Him, that glory may dwell in our land."
>
> From Proverbs 3:35: "The wise shall inherit glory,..."
>
> From 1 Peter 4:14: "If you are reproached for the name of Christ, blessed are you, for the Spirit of glory and of God rests upon you."
>
> And from Our Lord, Himself, again in John 17:22-23: "And the glory which You gave Me I have given them, that they may be one just as We are one: I in them, and You in Me; that they may be made perfect in one..."

In this last passage, Christ makes it abundantly clear that the outpouring of God's glory in our lives brings about unity – perfect unity – so that we can be "made perfect in one."

So let us take a moment to examine this concept of becoming "perfect in one".

As Christians, we are meant to be perfect in one – functioning as one person, one bride, one body that glorifies Christ and draws people out of darkness and into the light of His love. How often do we find this concept in the Bible – especially in the New Testament?

> From Romans 12:5: "For as we have many members in one body, but all the members do not have the same function, so we, being many, are one body in Christ, and individually members of one another."
>
> From 1 Corinthians 12:12: "For as the body is one and has many members, but all the members of that one body, being many, are one body, so also is Christ."

> From 1 Corinthians 12:24-27: "... But God composed the body... that there should be no schism in the body, but that the members should have the same care for one another. And if one member suffers, all the members suffer with it; or if one member is honored, all the members rejoice with it. Now you are the body of Christ, and members individually."

Yet, the Lord knew this journey to becoming one as the body of Christ – this effort to become His strong, glorious, beautiful, healthy bride – would not be an easy one and would require leadership from within the body itself.

Ephesians 4:12-13 explains that the five-fold ministry (apostles, prophets, evangelists, pastors, and teachers) is for equipping us as believers for the work of ministry and for the edifying of the body of Christ **until** "we all come to the unity of the faith and of the knowledge of the Son of God, to a perfect [person], to the measure of the stature of the fullness of Christ...."

While this is an extremely important passage in our current era, it is often emphasized differently than I am suggesting here.

Let's re-read the whole passage again starting from verse 11 for context and then dissect it further:

> From Ephesians 4:11-13: "And He himself gave some to be apostles, some prophets, some evangelists, and some pastors and teachers, for the equipping of the saints for the work of ministry, for the edifying of the body of Christ, till we all come to the unity of faith and of the knowledge of the Son of God, to a perfect man, to the measure of the stature of the fullness of Christ;"

Here we learn that the five-fold ministry has two distinct purposes:

1. "the equipping of the saints for the work of ministry"
2. "the edifying [building or constructing] of the body of Christ"

And that these ministries with their distinct purposes are time-bound. The five-fold ministries are to exist "till we all come to the unity of faith and of the knowledge of the Son of God."

Or as the Amplified Bible describes it, they are to exist "until we all attain oneness in the faith and in the comprehension of the [full and accurate] knowledge of the Son of God, that [we might arrive] at really mature manhood (the completeness of personality which is nothing less than the standard height of Christ's own perfection), the measure of the stature of the fullness of the Christ and the completeness found in Him." (AMP)

As believers, we are to literally "grow up" into the Body of Christ so that every part can work together effectively to cause additional growth – the addition of more believers. We will explore this further in the coming pages, but for now, let's make sure we catch the concept that the five-fold ministry of apostles, prophets, evangelists, teachers, and pastors is necessary and is set in the body of Christ to equip each of us for the work of ministry and to build us up into the body of Christ until we achieve unity of faith and of the knowledge of Christ.

So let us begin to rise to that level of maturity in Christ as individuals that we are not dependent upon the five-fold ministry, but rather are able to walk beside those in the five-fold ministry to develop others into their full maturity. Let us live at a level of individual maturity such that we operate together in ways that the world will experience us functioning as one and know that we are only able to do this because of His presence in our lives.

This is our ultimate collective destiny as believers – to live in such unity that we function as one – that we are "made perfect in one" – one body – one Bride – the Lamb's wife.

However, there is more to Christ's gift of glory than just unity. Are you prepared to dive deeper into what this gift grants to each of us?

"Authority," like many other words, has a wide application and is used with many shades of meaning. But Dr. Webster gives us, as its primary meaning, this short definition:

"Authority means a right to command."

…Now let us look for an authority that is supreme.… We cannot find such authority on earth. Every human Ruler, from the nursery to the throne, knows that his "right to command," i.e. his authority, is limited both in its degree and in its range. We must, therefore, look higher than to any human Ruler for that supreme authority… Such authority is found only in the living God.

- Shaler Granby Hillyer, in 1897, from the *Manual of Bible Morality*

Author of the *Manual of Bible Morality* and *Reminiscences of Georgia Baptists,*

Chair of Rhetoric and Professor of Theology at Mercer University,

One of the most highly respected Baptist preachers in Georgia for nearly 70 years during the 1800's

(and my third great-grandfather)

Chapter 4

The Power
The <u>Authority</u> from Glory Unleashed

According to John 17:23, in His prayer, Christ tells us the second reason for glory being given is "that the world may know You [God the Father] have sent Me [Your Son]."

We find here in Christ's own words that the manifestation of God's glory in our lives demonstrates to the world the authority of Christ being sent by God the Father. Yet perhaps one of the most interesting aspects of authority is the power that is automatically conferred upon those who are granted authority.

In fact, Christ begins his final words in Matthew with the statement that:

> "All authority has been given to Me in heaven and on earth." Matthew 28:18

And that statement is immediately followed by the Great Commission directive to:

> "Go therefore and make disciples of all the nations, baptizing them in the name of the Father and of the Son and of the Holy Spirit, teaching them to observe all things that I have commanded you…" Matthew 28:19-20a

Then He concludes these final words with the assurance that:

> "…I am with you always, even to the end of the age." Matthew 28:20b

As Christians, the Great Commission is essentially drilled into us (and for all the right reasons!), but I have found in my lifetime that little emphasis is put on the two statements Christ wrapped around the Great Commission:

1. All authority is already given to Him in heaven and on earth.
2. He is always with us.

These are shockingly powerful and unquestioningly definitive statements that leave no doubt as to:

- how much authority He has – ALL
- over what – HEAVEN AND EARTH
- and when He is available for us – ALWAYS

As the Body of Christ, have we forgotten these statements surrounding the Great Commission – these statements within which the Great Commission is embedded – that He has all authority in heaven and on earth, and that He is with us always?

These concepts that He is with us always and that He has all authority over heaven and earth are activated in our lives when His glory is upon us. As joint-heirs with Christ and because He gives us full access to the glory given to Him by God the Father, we are able to walk with Him in that same authority and with the power that His glory unleashes in our lives.

Consider 2 Corinthians 4:5-7:

> "For we do not preach ourselves, but Christ Jesus the Lord, and ourselves your bondservants for Jesus' sake. For it is the God who commanded light to shine out of darkness, who has shone in our hearts to give the light of the knowledge of the glory of God in the face of Jesus Christ. But we have this treasure in earthen vessels, that the excellence of the power may be of God and not of us."

This is not an abstract experience. Know that this is a very real and tangible experience that can and should happen regularly – eventually always – in our lives. God's glory should shine through us so that His power is manifest in the earth.

One powerful personal example comes to mind from when I lived in what is now South Sudan. At the time that it was the worst war zone in the world and my situation was in its most difficult moments, I occasionally wondered **how** I would get out alive, but I never wondered **if** I would get out alive. I never doubted that I would be well-cared for because I did not walk in fear. I knew the truth and, more importantly, I knew that I walked in the authority that comes with His glory. I knew according to Hebrews 13:5 that He would never leave me or forsake me. So I knew that He would never let anything happen to me unless it would bring greater glory to Him in the end. I knew I was right where I was supposed to be, walking in obedience to Him, and that meant He would take care of everything else around me.

Such amazing freedom is found in moments like that – to know the truth, to know that you are protected from harm, and to know that He has all authority to take care of the details! All we are required to do in those moments is trust and obey so that He is able to work out all that is happening in the situation. As a believer in Jesus Christ as your Lord and Savior, you can and absolutely should walk in that same authority every day with the peace and knowledge of being in His will.

Walking in this authority changes the atmosphere around you. People in the corporate world tell me that I have a unique charisma and that when I enter a room the atmosphere often seems to change. However, what they do not realize is that it is not me at all. It is Him with me. The shift that people sense is the hand of God upon me, His unmerited favor on my life, His glory surrounding me, and His presence in the room.

And the wonderful news is that it is there for you too. I am only walking in it, quite consciously and intentionally walking in it – His glory, the gift He has given each of us in the Body of Christ – and you should walk in it too. Every day. Let's look at a few verses describing the power of His presence to demonstrate and further assure us of how much authority is accessible through the gift of His glory:

> From Psalm 9:3: "When my enemies turn back, they shall fall and perish at Your presence."
>
> From Isaiah 59:19: "So shall they fear the name of the Lord from the west and His glory from the rising of the sun; when the enemy comes in like a flood, the Spirit of the Lord will lift up a standard against him."
>
> From Revelation 15:8: "The temple was filled with smoke from the glory of God and from His power…"

Clearly God's glory carries with it the commanding authority of heaven that unleashes His power on earth.

Now that we have discovered this, let's investigate the third reason for Christ's gift of His glory…

When representing man..., Paul speaks of him..., as "the image and glory of God." This investiture of authority gives him a likeness to God, the Supreme Ruler. In the state of innocence, man possessed this authority without fear from any of the creatures.... [T]he image of God is "renewed" in those who experience the regenerating influences of the Holy Spirit, and are created in Christ Jesus unto good works.

The word "renewed" carries back our thoughts to man's original state. A new creation is effected by the Spirit, restoring the regenerate to the knowledge, righteousness, and holiness from which man has fallen. In their renewed state, the effects of the fall still appear, and will remain until the last enemy, death, shall be destroyed; but their connection with the second Adam secures the completion of the good work begun, and assures them that they shall ultimately bear the likeness of the heavenly, who is the image of God.

- John Leadley (J. L.) Dagg, in 1857, from the *Manual of Theology* – the first comprehensive, systematic theology written by a Baptist in America

> Also the author of the *Manual of Theology Second Part: A Treatise on Church Order* written for the Baptist denomination as well as *Moral Science* and *Evidences of Christianity,*
>
> One of the most respected and profound thinkers in the Baptist Denomination,
>
> Third president of Mercer University,
>
> Soldier in the War of 1812
>
> (and my fourth great-grandfather)

Chapter 5

The Overflow
The <u>Testimony</u> of Lives Transformed

As John 17:23 comes to its end, Christ tells us the third purpose of the gift of His glory is so that humanity will know that God the Father loves them as much as He loves His own Son. Specifically, Christ says:

> "that the world may know that You... have loved them as You have loved Me."

As Christians – especially as Christians who walk with Christ in His glory, we are a testimony – a living witness to God the Father's love for the lost. When we receive and operate in the gift of His glory, we become the tangible evidence that God loves the world.

Let's dive a little deeper into the importance Christ placed upon people knowing of God the Father's love and then we will examine how glory's transformative power manifests itself in the natural world.

As we continue to review Christ's prayer in John 17, we realize that it is in fact the final recorded words He has with His Father before He goes to the garden of Gethsemane and is betrayed by Judas leading to His death, burial, and resurrection. Certainly this is an important passage of Scripture as we are given direct insight into Christ's final requests of God prior to the end of His time on earth. And what are those final requests?

We find His final seven requests throughout John 17:20-26.

The first three we have been discussing as the results of His gift of glory:

1. that we all may be one (unity)
2. that the world would know Jesus was sent by God (authority)
3. that the world would know God loves them
   as He loves Jesus (testimony)

The next two will be discussed further in chapter seven where we explore the activation of His glory in our daily lives:

4. that we may be with Jesus where He is
5. that we may behold Christ's glory given to Him by God

And the last two we will focus on for a few moments here as they are so closely tied to the third item of testimony above:

6. that the love with which God loved Jesus would be in us
7. that He would be in us

When Christ gifted us with His glory and as we choose to walk with Him in it, the world experiences the testimony that God loves them as He loves Jesus because of the granting of the sixth and seventh final requests of Christ – God's love is in us and Jesus is in us.

Consider that knowing the love of God for all humanity was so important to Christ that one of the primary final requests He made to God the Father was that we would be filled with God's love so that the world would know God's love for them. Not only was the purpose of His coming to demonstrate God's love, and not to condemn the world, as stated in John 3:16-17, "For God so loved the world that He gave His only begotten Son, that whoever believes in Him should not perish but have everlasting life. For God did not send His Son into the world to condemn the world, but that the world through Him might be saved.", but also this was the third and final purpose of His gift of glory to us upon His leaving. His glory allows us to overflow with His love to others because it literally oozes out of our spirit into the atmosphere around us resulting in the transformation of our lives and hopefully in the transformation of the lives of those around us.

This may seem a shocking statement to some, so let us examine three specific examples of how God's glory actually overflowed in a visible way through people in the Bible and reinforce those examples with specific verses indicating that this is the normal and expected outcome of experiencing God's glory.

Our first example is Moses, who spent a considerable amount of time in the presence of God's glory; however, we will look into just a couple situations where God's glory visibly transformed him in a way that others recognized.

Exodus 24:16 – 18 describes the scene as follows:

"Now the glory of the Lord rested on Mount Sinai, and the cloud covered it six days. And on the seventh day He called to Moses out of the midst of the cloud. The sight of the glory of the Lord was like a consuming fire on the top of the mountain in the eyes of the children of Israel. So Moses went into the midst of the cloud and went up into the mountain. And Moses was on the mountain forty days and forty nights."

Wow! Forty days and forty nights in the presence of the Lord's glory that appears as a consuming fire – that's going to transform you! It just is. We will see exactly how it transformed Moses in a few moments.

In Exodus 33:7 – 11, we have a scene where Moses puts up a tent far from the main camp of the Israelites so that he can meet with the Lord away from the people. When he goes into the tent, called the tabernacle of meeting, the cloud descends upon the doorway to the tent and the people can see it from afar, causing them to worship the Lord from their own tent doors. Then the Lord speaks directly with Moses "as a man speaks with his friend." This scene is followed in Exodus 33:12 – 23 by a glimpse into one of these conversations between Moses and the Lord where Moses asks that he see the Lord's glory. Yet the Lord explains that the full experience of seeing the glory of His face is too much for the human body to survive, so He will hide Moses while His glory passes by and then allow Moses to see His back.

And then we move into Exodus 34 where Moses receives the second set of tablets and, by the way, is again with the Lord for forty days and forty nights. Seriously, our physical bodies just are going to change if we spend forty days and nights in the direct presence of the Lord as Moses did, and in Exodus 34:29, we have the description of how Moses physical body was transformed by dwelling in the presence of the Lord's glory:

"... Moses did not know that the skin of his face shone while he talked with Him."

But apparently his skin did shine because both Aaron and the children of Israel were afraid to come near Moses. He eventually is able to meet with them and deliver the commandments given to him by the Lord, but then an interesting scene plays out in Exodus 34:33-35:

> "And when Moses had finished speaking with them, he put a veil on his face. But whenever Moses went in before the Lord to speak with Him, he would take the veil off until he came out; and he would come out and speak to the children of Israel whatever he had been commanded. And whenever the children of Israel saw the face of Moses, that the skin of Moses' face shone, then Moses would put the veil on his face again, until he went in to speak with Him."

Fascinating! God's glory transformed Moses' natural body to the point that his skin shined so brightly he had to wear a veil in the presence of the people during the normal course of his day so that they would be able to tolerate interacting with him.

Our second example is Saul, later to be renamed Paul. Having recently stood around guarding the clothes of those stoning Stephen and having consented to Stephen's death according to Acts 7:58 and Acts 8:1, Saul appears in Acts 9:1 "still breathing threats and murder against the disciples of the Lord," and heads to Damascus with the papers to detain and bring any Christians he finds to Jerusalem. However, he is getting ready to run straight into God's glory and it is going to stop him in his tracks – literally.

In Acts 9:3-5, we have the description of the scene when Saul experiences God's glory:

> "As he journeyed he came near Damascus and suddenly a light shone around him from heaven. Then he fell to the ground, and heard a voice saying to him, 'Saul, Saul, why are you persecuting Me?' And he said, 'Who are You, Lord?' Then the Lord said, 'I am Jesus, whom you are persecuting....'"

Saul, now known as Paul, also describes these moments and the effect of God's glory in his own words in Acts 22:11:

> "And since I could not see for the glory of that light, being led by the hand of those who were with me, I came to Damascus."

And in Acts 9:9, we have a more full description of the physical effect that experiencing God's glory has on Saul's body:

> "And he was three days without sight, and neither ate nor drank."

So Saul is blind and goes three days without eating or drinking. Think about that – three days without eating is not that bad. Many have done that for any number of reasons, but three days without drinking? Something has seriously been transformed in your physical body if you do not drink for three days. And everyone around him knew something had happened – the men with him had to lead him by the hand to Damascus and he was suddenly blind and not eating or drinking.

Then the big transformation happens – Ananias visits him, lays hands on him, something like scales fall from Saul's eyes, he can see again, he goes and gets baptized, he starts eating (and I assume drinking), spends time with the disciples (wasn't he going to arrest them and bring them back to Jerusalem?), and then according to Acts 9:20:

> "Immediately he preached the Christ in the synagogues, that He is the Son of God."

What?!? This guy was just standing around "consenting" to the stoning of a believer in Christ and making "havoc of the church" in the previous chapter and now he is preaching Christ – and not preaching Christ in the streets, but preaching Christ in the synagogues! Clearly his life was transformed with an incredible testimony when he met Jesus and experienced His glory.

Our third example is Jesus, himself, when he goes up on the mountain to pray in Luke 9:28-32:

> "Now it came to pass... that He took Peter, John, and James and went up on the mountain to pray. As He prayed, the appearance of His face was altered, and His robe became white and glistening.... But Peter and those with him were heavy with sleep; and when they were fully awake, they saw His glory..."

In this snapshot, we see that Christ begins the scene with what we would consider a normal human appearance, but as He prays, His glory begins to be revealed to the extent that His face changes and even His clothes are transformed.

You may wonder if these experiences – some would say supernatural experiences – are reserved only for heroes of the Bible, but know that our lives are also meant to be transformed into the same overflow of His love and transformed even in physical ways when we experience His glory. Not only do we have the examples of real people from the Bible to confirm this, but we also have the assurance of several passages throughout the Scriptures. For our purposes now, let's look at just one passage. It is rather long, but it is key to crystallizing the points and relevance of the prior examples.

From 2 Corinthians 3:7-18:

> "But if the ministry of death, written and engraved on stones, was glorious, so that the children of Israel could not look steadily at the face of Moses because of the glory of his countenance, which glory was passing away, how will the ministry of the Spirit not be more glorious?
>
> For if the ministry of condemnation had glory, the ministry of righteousness exceeds much more in glory.
>
> For even what was made glorious had no glory in this respect, because of the glory that excels. For if what is passing away was glorious, what remains is much more glorious. Therefore, since we have such hope, we use great boldness of speech – unlike Moses, who put a veil over his face so that the children of Israel could not look steadily at the end of what was passing away. But their minds were blinded. For until this day the same veil remains unlifted in the reading of the Old Testament, because the veil is taken away by Christ. But even to this day, when Moses is read, a veil lies on their heart.
>
> Nevertheless when one turns to the Lord, the veil is taken away.
>
> Now the Lord is the Spirit; and where the Spirit of the Lord is, there is liberty. But we all, with unveiled face, beholding as in a mirror the glory of the Lord, are being transformed into the same image from glory to glory, just as by the Spirit of the Lord."

We learn a few important points from this passage:

- the glory that Moses experienced and that required him to have a veiled face in front of the children of Israel was based on the Old Testament law – written on stones – a ministry of death and condemnation

- the glory that we experience through Christ's ministry of righteousness exceeds that former glory
- Christ lifts the veil that would prevent us from directly experiencing His glory
- the Spirit of the Lord grants us liberty or freedom to reflect the glory of the Lord without a veiled face
- we are being transformed directly into the image we are reflecting – from reflected glory to actual glory by the Spirit of the Lord

So the recognizable transformation of our lives is the normal and expected outcome of experiencing His glory, and this transformation becomes a testimony to the world of God's love for them.

Now that we better understand the three reasons for Christ sharing His glory with us:

1. Unity – that we all may be one
2. Authority – that the world will know God sent Him
3. Testimony – that the world will know God loves them
   just as He loves His Son

Let's pause for a moment to clear up what some may consider to be an interesting paradox in Scripture regarding Christ's ability to gift us with His glory…

… I am glad of an opportunity to say a good word for the old Book. It has proved itself a true friend. I have often put it to the test, and it has never failed me. To me it is God's word, and it has proved itself infallible…. I would invite your attention [to] the remarkable unity in diversity which characterizes the Bible. This fact, as I shall show, argues that there is but one author of the book and, of necessity, that this author is God….

Yes, the Bible is perfectly unique. There is not another book on earth like it, nor is it like any other book. Indeed, it is not one book, but a library of 66 books composed by 40 different writers from all ranks of society, and requiring at least 1,500 years in its composition….

Yet throughout this Book there is a marvelous unity. Though it was written by these different men from almost every walk of life, and, though it was 1,500 years in the making, it is, nevertheless, a harmonious whole. One spirit breathes through it all; one great ideal and purpose shines with ever-increasing brightness from its beginning to its end.

Though in 66 divisions, the Bible is one Book. Why? There is but one answer to the question. The answer is because the Holy Spirit of the Living God was the real Author!

… The Bible is a glorious temple of truth, with its broad foundations in Genesis, its majestic columns rising in the record of patriarch, prophet, and priest, its roof-tree in the Gospels of Jesus Christ, and its majestic dome in the Revelation of a New Heaven and New Earth wherein will dwell righteousness. The miraculous unity of the Book argues conclusively to the thoughtful mind the oneness and divinity of its origin and, therefore, its infallibility.

- John Roach Straton, in 1924, from *The Famous New York Fundamentalist-Modernist Debates: The Orthodox Side*

> Nationally known fundamentalist pastor of the famous Calvary Baptist Church in New York,
>
> Defender of Aimee Semple McPherson nationally from the pulpit during her trial,
>
> Experienced a Pentecostal outpouring of the Holy Spirit at his flagship Baptist church in New York City and began holding healing services there and around the country
>
> (and my great-grandfather)

Chapter 6
The Paradox – Isaiah 42:8

An interesting passage is found in Isaiah 42:8 and any exploration of God's glory requires some evaluation of this passage. For I have heard it spoken from the pulpit by at least one well-known minister that "God shares His glory with no one." I can only assume that this comment is referring specifically to this passage in Isaiah 42, and it is true that if taken out of the context of the passage and read solely on its own, then that one verse – Isaiah 42:8 most definitely says "My glory I will not give to another".

However, in any evaluation of the Scriptures, it is important to read not only a verse by itself, but also the context of the verse. Certainly situations exist in which a verse can be pulled out and stands on its own, yet often a verse is better evaluated in the context of the passage into which it was written and in the context of the overarching whole of how its concept fits within the Bible.

John 3:16 "For God so loved the world that He gave His only begotten Son, that whoever believes in Him should not perish but have everlasting life." is an example of the former. This verse stands on its own – immovable, immutable, and unshakeable – in any situation, anywhere in the world, for all eternity. That is why it is often one of the first verses we teach new Christians and often is the verse that brings people into their salvation experience with Christ. However, most verses require additional inquiry and a more holistic understanding of the scriptures that support them. Isaiah 42:8 is just such an example of this.

We know that God is consistent, so how do we address what could be considered a paradox between His words in Isaiah 42:8 and Christ's prayer in John 17:22?

When considering these two passages, they seem at first glance impossible to reconcile. How can God the Father say in Isaiah "I am the Lord, that is My name; and My glory I will not give to another," and then Jesus turn around and say in His prayer to God the Father "And the glory which You gave Me I have given them."?

These two passages could be considered so wholly opposed to each other as to create an insurmountable paradox in the mind of the reader. However, to overcome this potential paradox, one must look at the context of Isaiah 42, just as we have explored the context of John 17 earlier in this book. Let's take a few moments to do that in order to reassure ourselves that God is not inconsistent.

We must begin with a full reading of Isaiah 42:1-9 so that we can have a general sense of the passage and a specific understanding of Isaiah 42:8 in context:

Section 1 – Isaiah 42:1-4:

"Behold! My Servant whom I uphold, My Elect One in whom My soul delights! I have put My Spirit upon Him; He will bring forth justice to the Gentiles. He will not cry out, nor raise His voice, nor cause His voice to be heard in the street. A bruised reed He will not break, and smoking flax He will not quench; He will bring forth justice for truth. He will not fail or be discouraged, till He has established justice in the earth; and the coastlands shall wait for His law."

Section 2 – Isaiah 42:5-9:

Thus says God the Lord, Who created the heavens and stretched them out, Who spread forth the earth and that which comes from it, Who gives breath to the people on it, and spirit to those who walk on it: "I, the Lord, have called You as a covenant to the people, as a light to the Gentiles, to open blind eyes, to bring out prisoners from the prison, those who sit in darkness from the prison house. I am the Lord, that is My name; and My glory I will not give to another, nor My praise to carved images. Behold, the former things have come to pass, and new things I declare; before they spring forth I tell you of them."

Breaking Isaiah 42:1-9 into two distinct sections – verses 1-4 and verses 5-9, as I have done above, allows the reader to better understand what is happening in this scene.

In Section 1, God the Father is introducing His "Servant", also called His "Elect One", and describing how delighted He is with Him, how God has put His Spirit on Him, how He will bring forth justice to the Gentiles, and how He will establish justice in the earth. This is so obviously a description of God introducing His Son, Jesus Christ, that it is virtually unquestioned in biblical circles. There is literally no other being who fits the description of the Person whom God describes in these verses, except Jesus Christ. So we will proceed in our exploration of the passage with the understanding that, in verses 1-4, God is introducing and describing His Son, Jesus Christ.

In Section 2, God the Father is briefly described in verse 5 and then He turns and speaks to His Son whom He has just introduced in the prior verses. We know that He is clearly speaking to the One whom He has just introduced because He uses conversational language that would be used between two people. For example, He says "I, the Lord, have called You" and "I will keep You and give You as a covenant to the people". With this understanding that Section 2, specifically verses 6-9, is a glimpse into God the Father speaking to His Son, verse 8 makes much more sense when compared with John 17:22.

In fact, Isaiah 42:8 then becomes the foundational and supporting reference for Christ's words in John 17:22. A very rough, yet much more modern and perhaps understandable, rendering of Isaiah 42:6-8 would be something like "I am God the Father and I have called You – My Son Jesus Christ – in righteousness and I am going to hold Your hand and keep You and give You as a covenant to people and as a light to sinners so that the blind will see and people living in darkness will come out of the darkness and be set free. I am God the Father and I am not going to give My glory to anyone else but You, My Son. I am not giving My glory to some other being than You and I am not giving My praise to carved images or idols."

To me, a reading of the passage in the way described above makes much more sense given all the other verses in the Bible where God's glory is referenced and especially helps to reconcile Christ's words in John 17.

Rest assured, be at peace, and know beyond any doubt that God is not inconsistent. We know, based on Christ's words in John 17:22, that God did in fact give His glory to His Son, Jesus Christ. Given the glimpse that we have of Christ's prayer to His Father in John 17 regarding His glory, isn't it also possible, perhaps some would say likely, that we are given a similar glimpse in Isaiah 42 of God explaining to His Son that He – God the Father – is not giving His glory to anyone else, "to another", except His Son?

My hope is that this will also help you to reconcile what otherwise might be quite a paradox if taken out of context. And now let's begin to discover how we activate this amazing gift of His glory in our lives...

The tragedy of the Christian Church is that we are always hoping someone else will do the work. But it is going to take you and me to do the job, along with thousands of others whom Christ is calling to surrender their whole lives to this cause.

- Jack McAlister

    Founder of World Literature Crusade, now Every Home for Christ, in 1946,

    Famous Prayer Warrior and Activator of Prayer Warriors globally,

    A dear friend, inspirer, and mentor – really looking forward to seeing "Uncle" Jack in heaven along with so many others

    (and my third cousin)

Chapter 7

The Activation
Walking in His Glory Every Day

Genesis 3:8 tells us that, after the fall, Adam and Eve "hid themselves from the presence of the Lord God..." yet this very being with Him in His presence is what He seeks to experience with us.

This is the separation that He has been seeking to reconcile through all of time so that it will not exist for eternity. This separation from His presence is what prevents us from living in the fullness of all that He has for us. His desire is that we live in His presence all day, every day, for all eternity. Think through this carefully. If it were not so, then why would God the Father send His only Son to provide the way for us to have eternal life in His presence.

Yet on earth we have the option every day – to walk in His presence and allow His glory to surround us – or to walk outside of His presence in our own intellectual capacity and wisdom. So often we choose the second option because the busy-ness of our days pulls us from the eternal perspective into the temporal perspective. His desire is to use us – as His Body, His Bride – to break through with the eternal into the temporal as light and life and glory for all to see and be drawn to His power and love.

And this is something you can do without leaving your current job or career. You have the ability to walk in His glory no matter where you are or what you are doing.

Walking in God's glory does not require that you be called to a certain role in "church ministry" – that you become a full-time pastor, evangelist, or missionary. (If you do feel called to those professions, that is wonderful and the world certainly needs you! However, being in that profession is not a prerequisite to sharing His glory with the world.)

Walking in His glory only requires that you surrender yourself daily to Him so that His glory can shine through you. In order to walk in His glory every day, one must have a relationship with Him every day. It is virtually impossible to share in the glory that surrounds Him and His throne if you are not able to be near Him and have access to His throne.

Beyond the "why" – for unity, authority, and testimony – and the "who" – each of us who believes in Christ – that we covered in the first five chapters, let's finish by considering the other three logistics of His glory – what, where, and how.

What is His glory?

Let's take a moment to step back and examine what exactly His glory is before we continue forward into where and how to access it.

We should understand that the word translated as "glory" in the Old Testament is the Hebrew word *kabod* (K-B-D) and in the New Testament is the Greek word *doxa*. The best full rendering of these two words, kabod and doxa, that I can offer is something along the lines of:

– the heavy weight and honor of God's presence, good opinion, and splendor

This rendering combines the more literal translation of kabod and the developed translation of doxa that appears to have happened as Hebrew Scriptures from the Old Testament were translated to Greek and then Greek was more prevalently used for the New Testament. Also, this rendering of the meaning or description of "glory" holds to be consistent with the experience of God's glory described throughout the Bible and, frankly, with my personal experiences of it. But let's double-check to make sure this definition is consistent with what we know about God's glory before we proceed to accept it:

- God's glory has weight to it and is often "heavy" sometimes displaying itself as a cloud
- God's glory does demonstrate the honor of His presence
- God's glory does indicate His good opinion of those who walk in it
- God's glory does manifest itself as His splendor

Therefore, I have found this definition to be the best way to describe the substance of His glory: the heavy weight and honor of God's presence, good opinion, and splendor.

Imagine if we were able to walk in that substance all the time. The world would take notice and we could point them to Him!

And that is the key to being gifted with His glory. It is entrusted to us for all the reasons we explored earlier: unity, authority, and testimony and with the expectation that it will be used for pointing others to Him. You see this is all about Him and not at all about us because only He is worthy of all power, honor, glory, and praise. In fact in John 8:50, Jesus says, "I do not seek My own glory", so even He was not seeking glory for Himself. He was only seeking glory in order to show people His Father's love.

So with the more clear definition of what God's glory is and the understanding that it is entrusted to us so that we can point others to Him, let's continue to move forward with where we can always find it and how it is activated in our lives.

Where do we find His glory?

Throughout the Bible we see it in the wilderness with the Israelites, in the temple, scattered among the Psalms, in the visions of Ezekiel, described as covering the earth like the seas in Habakkuk, on Christ in the Gospels, being seen by Stephen and Paul in Acts, mentioned in various other books throughout the New Testament, and greatly depicted in Revelation.

However, we cannot be chasing all over the Bible or the universe trying to find it when we are meant to be walking in it daily. So Christ made a way for it to be very accessible in one consistent, unchangeable place that we can access anytime, anywhere.

Curious as to where that is? It is at His throne. Ezekiel sees this several times, and from personal experience, the one place where I know that no matter what is happening I can find Him and experience His glory is at His throne. When our spirit lives in His presence, before His throne, we have full accessibility to Him and His glory at all times.

While your mind takes a while to register that fact, let's explore some passages that support our ability to do that.

First, let's begin with Christ's own words as we go back to His fourth and fifth final requests – the ones we skipped over in Chapter Five. Christ continues His list of final requests with John 17:24:

"Father, I desire that they also whom You gave Me may be with Me where I am, that they may behold My glory which You have given Me;"

Our traditional church teaching has indicated that this is more about Heaven to be experienced upon our physical death. However, there is nothing in the words of Christ that indicate it was not meant to be present tense, nothing to indicate that we cannot be in His presence, where He is now and behold His glory.

To further support this, we have the fact that at the moment of Christ's death on the cross, the veil that separated the Holy of Holies in the temple was ripped from top to bottom, becoming physical evidence that the Holy of Holies – the place where God and His glory dwelt on earth and symbolic of the place where God and His glory dwell in Heaven – was now readily accessible to all.

Second, let's look at David. He was in and out of the throne room of heaven all the time. He danced before the Lord. He entered the gates with thanksgiving and the courts with praise according to Psalm 100:4, but perhaps David's most telling description is found in Psalm 27:4:

"One thing have I asked of the Lord, that will I seek, inquire for, and [insistently] require: that I may dwell in the house of the Lord [in His presence] all the days of my life, to behold and gaze upon the beauty [the sweet attractiveness and the delightful loveliness] of the Lord and to meditate, consider, and to inquire in His temple." (AMP)

David understood what it meant to dwell in the presence of the Lord before His throne and he clearly states that was for all the days of his life, not just after his physical death.

Third, we could look at Ezekiel, who was regularly seeing the Lord on His throne in Heaven, but for the sake of time and variety, let's look at Stephen next. In Acts 7:55-56, after Stephen has preached truth to the high priest and the council of elders, who are "cut to the heart" by his words, we learn that Stephen, "being full of the Holy Spirit, gazed into heaven and saw the glory of God, and Jesus standing at the right hand of God, and said, 'Look! I see the heavens opened and the Son of Man standing at the right hand of God!'" Then they took him out of the city to be stoned. So Stephen saw into heaven and saw the glory of God surrounding Jesus while he was very much alive.

Fourth, let's look at the verse that helped me to best accept that this was a normal place for my spirit to be and that granted me the confidence to enter into His presence at any time without fear, doubt, or hesitation. We will look at the first part of Hebrews 4:16 in three different translations to reinforce its message.

> From the Amplified: "Let us then fearlessly and confidently and boldly draw near to the throne of grace (the throne of God's unmerited favor to us sinners)," (AMP)

> From the New Living Translation: "So let us come boldly to the throne of our gracious God," (NLT)

> From the New King James Version: "Let us therefore come boldly to the throne of grace,"

Process this for a while also – it would actually be more strange if our spirit was not able to move in and out of the throne room with ease and confidence because we are joint-heirs with the King of Kings destined to rule and reign with Him for eternity. So it is probably a good idea to become comfortable with being around His throne and in His presence.

Now don't get weird about that. We are not all going to start running around on earth now with royal tiaras and scepters of gold. Just be normal about it because this is our destiny as the Bride, the Lamb's wife.

As you get more comfortable with this concept, you will find that it feels very natural and normal for your spirit to be praying at His feet before His throne, praising and worshiping at His throne, and talking with Him there. Just enter in. After all, He is your friend and you are part of the Body that will become His Bride.

How do we activate His glory?

So now that we know where to find His glory, let's consider how we activate it in our lives on earth so that we get the expected results of unity, authority, and testimony that demonstrate God's love to the world. Again we look to the Scriptures to help us with this.

For our purposes right now, we are going to explore four simple ways to activate His glory in our lives:

1. Ask for your inheritance. That's right – just ask for the Lord to pour out your inheritance of His glory on your life. Here are two verses to support that this is your inheritance as a child of God:

   From Ephesians 1:17-21, we have a prayer from Paul: "that the God of our Lord Jesus Christ, the Father of glory, may give to you the spirit of wisdom and revelation in the knowledge of Him, the eyes of your understanding being enlightened; that you may know what is the hope of His calling, what are the riches of the glory of His inheritance in the saints, and what is the exceeding greatness of His power toward us who believe, according to the working of His mighty power which He worked in Christ when He raised Him from the dead and seated Him at His right hand in the heavenly places, far above all principality and power and might and dominion, and every name that is named, not only in this age but also in that which is to come."

   From Proverbs 3:35: "The wise shall inherit glory," and I have to believe that those who choose Jesus are very wise. Therefore, this verse further demonstrates that glory is our inheritance as believers in Christ.

2. Pray. This seems pretty obvious, but we are looking for the simple things that result in His glory being manifest. Sometimes we over-complicate things when the simple, obvious answer is the best one. So pray – pray the glory of heaven into the earth.

   Let's use an example we already discovered in Luke 9 where Jesus went up on the mountain to pray. In that example, we are told that Jesus prayed and the glory of God began to be manifest through the altering of the appearance of His face and through His robe becoming white and glistening. Due to these supernatural results, I have to believe that in those moments of prayer He touched the throne room of heaven and God's glory began to flow over Him. So we should pray in that way – where we go before God's throne boldly according to Hebrews 4:16 and literally pray heaven into the earth.

   We have a model for beginning this kind of prayer in the Lord's Prayer found in Matthew 6:9-10: "Our Father in heaven, hallowed be Your name, Your kingdom come, Your will be done, on earth as it is in heaven." That's a wonderful start and keep going from there!

3. Seek things above, allowing Christ to encompass you in all that you do. By remaining focused on heaven's perspective – even in your daily life, you can stay hidden in Christ with the result being that others see Him and His glory when they see you. Colossians 3:1-4 states, "If you were raised with Christ, seek those things which are above, where Christ is, sitting at the right hand of God. Set your mind on things above, not on things on the earth. For you died, and your life is hidden with Christ in God. When Christ who is our life appears, then you also will appear with Him in glory."

4. Rejoice. Proverbs 28:12 tells us, "When the righteous rejoice, there is great glory," so spend time praising, worshiping, and rejoicing. Frankly, I have found that this is one of the most powerful ways to activate His glory in my life. Just a few minutes of rejoicing, singing, praising, and worshiping results in an immediate change in my perspective and the atmosphere around me.

As a final comment on activating His glory in your life, be aware that just as God's glory can be activated, it can also be deactivated or rejected. Consider Jeremiah 2:11, where God states, "But My people have changed their Glory for what does not profit." This was an action that the people took to reject or deactivate His glory in their life, and God was not happy about it. In fact, He was extremely unhappy about it.

Please do not do that – do not reject or ignore this precious gift that Christ has given you. Please consider pausing as you finish reading this book and beginning now to activate His glory in your life. Even do that in this moment with a simple prayer such as the following:

Father God, in the name of Jesus, as Your beloved child I come before You boldly and ask for the inheritance of Your glory to be poured out through my life so that others will know You and the love You have for them.

Or the following – (a favorite of mine when I am feeling a bit exhausted and like I am running on empty):

Jesus, let others see You when they see me.

There is no formula or specific prayer to be said or song to be sung. Just begin to use the ways described in Scripture as you continue to mature in your ability to live continuously in His presence.

As we walk individually in God's glory made available to us as a gift from Jesus, we will begin to truly function as a "body" united with each other and with Christ as the Head in a way that will bring untold glory to Him so that millions, perhaps billions, more will know Him and His unquestioning, unconditional love for them.

If we are going to come into the full, mature Body of Christ that is meant to be His Bride – the Bride for whom He will return, each of us must take hold of living continually in His presence, walking in full obedience to Him, and radiating His glory in the earth.

The very kindergarten truth of Christianity is that we must be born again. That is the beginning of all else.... 'Ye must be born again.' This is the ultimatum of heaven, and on no ground whatsoever is it possible to get by it. It is final. It is fundamental.... Out of the heart are issues of life, and until hearts of stone and sin are taken out of us, and hearts of flesh to love God are put into us we cannot please God nor walk worthily before our fellow men....

Jesus did not say, 'Ye must be reformed again," but He did say, 'Ye must be born again." Again He said, 'Except a man be born again, he cannot see the Kingdom of God.' He cannot even 'see it!' And yet some are imagining that we can bring in the Kingdom merely by righteous laws and improved social and economic conditions!

We need the old-fashioned truth of regeneration as the bases of all our thinking. It is a truth great enough to serve as the foundation for our entire philosophy of life.

- John Roach Straton, in 1925, from *Old Gospel at the Heart of the Metropolis*

> Nationally known fundamentalist pastor of the famous Calvary Baptist Church in New York City with prior pastorates in Chicago, Baltimore, and Norfolk,
>
> Installed the first church-owned radio station in the United States,
>
> Defender of Aimee Semple McPherson nationally from the pulpit during her trial,
>
> Experienced a Pentecostal outpouring of the Holy Spirit at his flagship Baptist church in New York City and began holding healing services there and around the country
>
> (and my great-grandfather)

Chapter 8

The Evidence
A Final Word about Glory & Fulfilling Our Mission

Romans 3:23 states, "for all have sinned and fall short of the glory of God,"

This verse is perhaps one of the most quoted verses in evangelism to help the lost realize they are sinners, and we often reference it in the church to remind ourselves that each of us is also a sinner saved by grace. However, I have found very little emphasis upon the second half of the verse "all... fall short of the glory of God."

Apparently these two concepts – all have sinned and all fall short of the glory of God – are, in some way, of interconnected importance to the Lord. He spends a significant portion of His last words on earth to His Father focusing on the importance of glory being given to us and us being able to have and behold it.

Yet it is not only in the one verse of Romans that we find salvation and glory to be intertwined. Consider the following passages also:

> From 2 Thessalonians 2:13-14: "But we are bound to give thanks to God always for you, brethren beloved by the Lord, because God from the beginning chose you for salvation through sanctification by the Spirit and belief in truth, to which He called you by our gospel, for the obtaining of glory of our Lord Jesus Christ."

> From 2 Corinthians 4:3-4: "But even if our gospel is veiled, it is veiled to those who are perishing, whose minds the god of this age has blinded, who do not believe, lest the light of the gospel of the glory of Christ, who is the image of God, should shine on them."

> From Psalm 85:9: "Surely His salvation is near to those who fear Him, that glory may dwell in our land."

> From Ephesians 1:7-12: "In Him we have redemption through His blood, the forgiveness of sins, according to the riches of His grace which He made to abound toward us in all wisdom and prudence, having made known to us the mystery of His will, according to His good pleasure,

which He purposed in Himself, that in the dispensation of the fullness of the times He might gather together in one all things in Christ, both which are in heaven and which are on earth – in Him. In Him also we have obtained an inheritance being predestined according to the purpose of Him who works all things according to the counsel of His will that we who first trusted in Christ should be to the praise of His glory."

This collection of verses demonstrates that salvation is intricately connected with God's glory. They are meant to go hand-in-hand with each other. As we are redeemed from sin, we are also given the ability to be truly transformed in our born-again nature by His glory becoming evident in our lives.

For the glory of God is the evidence of God in our lives – that we are His and we belong to Him. His glory is a sign and confirmation of His presence that brings His power to His people on earth. However, the significance of this may have been lost over time with a focus on other aspects of our Christian life.

With the more full understanding of the significance of being able to walk in His glory presented in this short book, my hope and prayer is that we will take hold of the unique opportunity we have in our generation to fulfill our mission together and truly become one body – the Bride of Christ – the Lamb's wife – that functions with authority and demonstrates God's love for the world.

Join me and others in His presence – it's a beautiful place to live and there is much to be done for Him!

Then the Lord said:
"...truly, as I live, all the earth shall be filled
with the glory of the Lord..."
Numbers 14:20-21

For the earth will be filled with the knowledge of the glory of the Lord,
as the waters cover the sea.
Habakkuk 2:14

And the Word became flesh and dwelt among us,
and we beheld His glory, the glory as of the only begotten of the Father,
full of grace and truth.
John 1:14

...being confident of this very thing,
that He who has begun a good work in you will complete it
until the day of Jesus Christ....
Only let your conduct be worthy of the gospel of Christ, so that...
you stand fast in one spirit, with one mind
striving together for the faith of the gospel...
Philippians 1:6

Now to Him
who is able to keep you from stumbling and to present you faultless
before the presence of His glory with exceeding joy,
to God our Savior, who alone is wise,
be glory and majesty, dominion and power,
both now and forever.
Amen.
Jude 24-25

A Few Words about the Quotes between the Chapters

As one can guess from the authors of the various quotes between the chapters in this book, I was born into a very strong family line of ministry - actually several family lines. When we receive Christ as our Lord and Savior, we are each grafted into the Body of Christ and become joint-heirs with Him in His royal family line; however, during our earthly lives, we are also born into or adopted into natural family lines. This is most often not of our choosing as these decisions are usually made for us well before we are conscious of the natural family to which we belong.

The family names of Dagg, Hillyer, McAlister, and Straton have at various times been so well known in the earth as to have their lives, sermons, and books used to teach university and seminary students and to have been written about by people ranging from John Foxe in "Foxe's Book of Martyrs" to John Knox in "The History of the Reformation of Scotland" to David du Plessis, a founder of the charismatic movement who was known as "Mr. Pentecost". Frankly, I am slightly baffled and completely humbled by God allowing me to be born into this great family of ministers and missionaries - true world-changers - who have significantly and successfully impacted the Body of Christ over at least the last four and a half centuries among various denominations and throughout the world, but He did see fit for me to be a part of this family... and so I am.

With that unchangeable fact and with the knowledge of my deep family roots, I have felt compelled at times throughout my life and in varying degrees of urgency to express myself in ministry as well - sometimes in the mission field, occasionally in the guest pulpit, and - more often - behind the scenes. However, now the time has come and the compulsion is so strong that I must begin to share openly with the Body of Christ that which I feel has been entrusted to me and flows out of me or risk disobedience to the Lord. My prayer is that what flows out of me - the overflow or testimony of His glory - such as the content of this short book - will be a great blessing in the earth and will bring great glory to Him.

I have seen and experienced much of the worst and, thankfully, much of the best that this world has to offer and I can say unequivocally throughout it all that I have chosen, do choose, and always will choose Jesus above all else. I am by no means perfect and those who know me well - my family, my friends, those who work with me, those who have worked for me, and those for whom I have worked - can definitely testify to all of my daily faults and failures. Yet through it all I have always known that He is with me - by my side - protecting, guarding, and most importantly guiding me. My heart is to follow Him, to daily walk with Him, and to live in obedience to Him in order to ultimately fulfill His high call for my life in this generation.

As at least the seventh-known successive generation of my family lines to serve the Lord and the Body of Christ in ministry throughout the earth, I count the blessing of the natural family lines into which I was born to be an incredible honor, an inexplicable privilege, and a tremendous responsibility - yet it is not a great weight of responsibility, but rather a great joy. My hope is that you have also experienced great joy in reading a few of the quotes from these amazing people who have gone before me and that, in reading their comments, you will see the pattern and thread of all that Christ wants to do in the earth at this time and through His Bride - you and me and all the others who have chosen Him.

Thank you so much for taking the time - your valuable time - to read this book!

May it be a blessing to you and an encouragement for you to bless others in all that you do!

In His service,

Julia Eileen McLaughlin

About the Author

Julia Eileen McLaughlin holds a Bachelor of Science in International Business from Oral Roberts University as well as a Masters of Business Administration in Global Technology Management from American Intercontinental University. In her more than 20-year corporate career, she has led several organizations and trained thousands of people at numerous companies on topics ranging from negotiations to project management to software for accounting, financial systems, and hospital claims billing. With her experience in technology implementation and operations management, she has been instrumental in helping the companies she has worked for win or retain contracts with numerous top-tier clients including JPMorgan Chase, Wal-Mart/Sam's Clubs, Bank of America, Kaiser Permanente, Fidelity Investments, Tenet Healthcare Corporation, AT&T, and the Department of Defense. She has also been an invited guest speaker for the University of South Florida's Management Information Systems program, the United States Department of Defense's annual hospital business office conference, and IBM's Global Smarter Commerce Summit as well as a panelist and presenter at other events.

Her ministry work includes a brief career sabbatical from December 2000 through early 2001 to do volunteer missions work and live in southern Sudan (now officially South Sudan) for four and a half months. This life-changing experience gave her the opportunity to preach and teach the Bible almost daily while living in what was at that time the worst war zone in the world. As a result of this opportunity, she was invited to share her story during the student session of the National Missionary Convention in Tulsa, Oklahoma in 2001. She also served as the United States' Interim Executive Director of a small, non-profit organization that builds villages to care for African orphans and widows, and she had the great privilege of leveraging her business experience to provide consultative services to one of the top theological seminaries in the world.

Julia is a direct descendant of John Leadley Dagg, Shaler Granby Hillyer, John Leadley Dagg Hillyer, David Straton, Henry Dundas Douglas Straton, John Roach Straton, Warren Badenoch Straton, Harvey McAlister, Eileen McAlister Straton, and Cathleen Straton Sandidge – who were at various times in history well-known leaders in the Baptist, Presbyterian, and Assemblies of God denominations and, more recently, in the Pentecostal and Charismatic movements. As such, she is the seventh-known successive generation in her family lines to serve the Lord and the Body of Christ in ministry throughout the earth.

She was raised as an "interdenominational" Christian – Presbyterian at church, Charismatic Pentecostal at home, and often visited Assemblies of God, Baptist, and Methodist churches for special events. This upbringing allows her to view Christianity across all denominational barriers and doctrinal differences as one faith brought together in the Body of Christ according to the Word of God and the Holy Spirit – much as it was during the time of the early church. She has traveled to 30 countries – the first being Israel – on 4 continents and has spoken and taught at various venues around the world.

She lives in central Florida and can be reached at julia.eileen.mclaughlin@gmail.com
Her Twitter feed is @juliaeileen .

Made in the USA
Columbia, SC
27 July 2024

39470251R00039